Best Friends

by Holly Harper

illustrated by Kübra Teber

OXFORD
UNIVERSITY PRESS
AUSTRALIA & NEW ZEALAND

Liam and Danny were best friends. They sat together at school and liked all the same things.

Danny

Liam

"My family goes on holiday to Sandy Island every summer," Danny told Liam. "You should ask your parents if you can come, too."

Liam's parents said he could go on holiday with Danny.

"We're going to have so much fun!" said Danny.

When they arrived, Liam was excited to go on an adventure. "Let's go to the beach," he said.

"Hey Danny!" A girl was waving at Danny.

"It's so good to see you, Danny," she said.

"This is Poppy," Danny told Liam. "She's my best friend."

Liam was surprised. He thought *he* was Danny's best friend.

"Let's go exploring," said Poppy. "Race you to the beach!"

Danny and Poppy ran off, leaving Liam behind.

When Liam caught up to Poppy and Danny, they were searching the sand.

"What are you doing?" he asked Danny.

"We're looking for shells for our shell drawing collection," explained Danny. "We look for the rarest shells and draw them every year."

"We're searching for a storm snail shell,"
said Poppy.

Liam picked up a rainbow shell. It looked special.

"Is this it?" he asked.

Poppy laughed. "No, that's an oyster shell," she said. "We already have lots of those."

"Oh," said Liam. He dropped the shell he'd found, feeling useless.

Liam didn't think looking for shells was much fun.

"Let's do something else," he said. "Danny, why don't we go and read superhero comics?"

"I don't like superhero comics," said Poppy.

'I wasn't talking to you,' Liam thought.

The next day, Liam and Danny went body boarding. Liam was excited. He had never done it before.

Soon Poppy showed up.

Poppy was really good at body boarding, and so was Danny. Liam kept falling off.

Poppy and Danny laughed a lot, but Liam didn't think it was funny.

The next day Liam told Danny he had an idea.

"Let's do something *without* Poppy," he said.

"Why would we do that?" Danny asked. "She's my best friend."

There was a knock at the door. It was Poppy.

"Let's go play Waves," said Poppy.

"I don't know how to play," said Liam.

"It's easy and it's fun!" said Danny.

Poppy and Danny jumped over the tide.

Liam didn't understand the rules at all.

"That's ten points for Poppy, eight points for me, and zero points for you, Liam!" said Danny. "But don't worry. It's just a bit of fun."

"It's not fun!" Liam shouted. "Nothing has been fun since we got here, and it's all because of her!"

Liam stormed off.

Danny came over.

"That wasn't very nice," Danny said. "Poppy's my best friend."

"I thought *I* was your best friend though," said Liam.

"Both of you are my best friends," said Danny. "Maybe we could all be best friends!"

Liam felt awful for shouting. He walked back to Poppy.

"Hello, Poppy," he said. "I'm sorry for getting mad. I don't know about shells or how to body board or play Waves. I felt left out."

"I'm sorry we left you out," said Poppy. "We can teach you all those things."

Danny and Poppy taught Liam how to play Waves. It was fun when he knew the rules.

Next, they taught him how to body board. It was tricky at first, although he eventually got the hang of it. When he fell off, they all laughed together.

Danny and Poppy taught Liam the names of the shells.

"What colour is a storm snail shell?" asked Liam.

"Purple," Poppy said.

"Like this?" Liam said, holding up a shell.

"I don't believe it!" Danny gasped in amazement. "The rarest shell!"

Danny, Poppy and Liam went back to the house to add the storm snail shell to their shell drawing collection.

"There's just one more thing to add," said Poppy.

When it was time to leave, Danny and Liam gave Poppy a hug. Liam was going to miss his new best friend.

"See you next summer," said Liam. "It's going to be fun!"

Best friends forever
D, L & P